A History of Fashion and Costume

Volume 6
The Victorian Age

Peter Chrisp

☑® Facts On File, Inc.

The Victorian Age

Copyright © 2005 Bailey Publishing Associates Ltd

Produced for Facts On File by
Bailey Publishing Associates Ltd
11a Woodlands
Hove BN3 6TJ

Project Manager: Roberta Bailey
Editor: Alex Woolf
Text Designer: Simon Borrough
Artwork: Dave Burroughs, Peter Dennis,
Tony Morris
Picture Research: Glass Onion Pictures

Printed and bound in Hong Kong

Facts On File, Inc.
132 West 31st Street
New York NY 10001

Facts On File books are available at special
discounts when purchased in bulk quantities for
businesses, associations, institutions, or sales
promotions. Please call our Special Sales
Department in New York at 212/967-8800 or
800/322-8755.

You can find Facts On File on the World Wide
Web at: http://www.factsonfile.com

Library of Congress Cataloging-in-Publication Data

Chrisp, Peter.
A history of fashion and costume.
Volume 6, The Victorian Age/Peter
Chrisp.
 p. cm.
Includes bibliographical references and
 index.
 ISBN 0-8160-5949-7
 1. Clothing and dress—Great
Britain—History—19th century.
2. Clothing and dress—United
States—History—19th century.
3. Great Britain—History—Victoria,
1837–1901. I. Title: Victorian Age.
II. Title.
 GT737.C57 2005
 391'.00941—dc 22
2005040044

The publishers would like to thank
the following for permission to use
their pictures:

Art Archive: 6, 7, 8, 9, 11 (top), 16, 17
(both), 18, 21, 25, 26, 27, 33, 35
(right), 36, 38, 42, 45 (bottom), 46, 48,
50, 52, 53 (top), 56, 58
Bridgeman Art Library: 23, 24
Mary Evans Picture Library: 10, 11
(bottom), 14, 15 (bottom), 19, 20
(both), 31, 40, 45 (top), 53 (bottom),
57 (both), 59
Popperfoto: 37
Topham: 54
Victoria & Albert Museum: 15 (top),
22, 28, 30, 32, 35 (left), 39, 51, 55

Contents

Introduction

The British queen, Victoria, has given her name to the era between 1837 and 1901, the years of her reign, the longest of any British ruler. The Victorian era was a period of world as well as British history, for the queen ruled at a time when Britain had a vast global empire, including a quarter of the planet's population.

It was a time of massive social change. Railroads were built across America and Europe, where many new industries developed. Britain led the way in manufacturing, earning the nickname the "workshop of the world." The growth of British industries drew vast numbers of people from the countryside to rapidly growing towns and cities. Between 1837 and 1901, the population doubled, from 18.5 to 37 million. By 1901, three quarters of British people lived in towns and cities.

Clothing was transformed by factory production, and by new inventions such as the sewing machine. Cheap clothes could now be mass produced. The period saw the birth of a true fashion industry, with the first department stores, fashion magazines, and mail-order catalogs, allowing people living in Melbourne and San Francisco to follow the latest European styles.

Just as people have always done, the Victorians used clothes as a type of language, sending signals to others about their class, status, and attitudes. In the Victorian age, the language of clothing was understood by everybody, who could instantly place someone's social position by their dress. It was also international: in Moscow or New York, a Victorian gentleman could be recognized by his tall silk hat and gold-topped cane.

Chapter 1: Early Victorian Fashions

At the beginning of the nineteenth century, the clothes of men and women were simple and comfortable. Women wore light, white dresses, with waists that fell just below the bust. This allowed them to dress without corsets, which had been worn by women since the fifteenth century. Men wore knee breeches or close-fitting trousers, white shirts, waistcoats, and a coat with a cutaway front and two tails behind. This was originally an eighteenth-century riding outfit, designed to free the legs on horseback.

In 1823, when this picture of a London ball was made, women still wore loose, comfortable dresses.

As fashions changed in the early 1820s, the waist of dresses moved down to the real position of a woman's waist, allowing corsets, also called stays, to be worn again. For the rest of the century, all women would wear corsets. In the 1820s these were tightly laced to give a narrow waist, contrasting with puffed-out sleeves above and wider skirts below. Dresses now came in bright colors, decorated with stripes and floral patterns. Outdoors, women wore wide hats trimmed with feathers, flowers, and ribbons.

In the 1820s, men, like women, used artificial methods to change the shape of their bodies. Fashionable men, called dandies, padded their chests and shoulders and wore tight stays. An 1825 poem by Bernard Blackmantle declared, "Each lordly man his taper waist displays / Combs his sweet locks and laces on his stays."

Attitudes to Fashion

The nineteenth century was an age of satirical cartoons and writings—works poking fun at the foolishness of people's behavior. Satirists, like the cartoonist George Cruikshank, found plenty to make fun of in the changing fashions of the day, with the conceited dandies, and ladies with tiny waists. Throughout the Victorian age, every new fashion would be similarly mocked.

More than any previous people, the Victorians were aware of how fashions had changed over the course of history. Thanks to new public art galleries, people could see paintings of the rich in the strange-looking clothes of earlier centuries. This led to serious attacks on the very idea of following fashions. In 1882 the writer Oscar Wilde declared, "From the sixteenth century to our own day there is hardly any form of torture that has not been inflicted on girls, and endured by women, in obedience to ... unreasonable and monstrous Fashion."

The Victorians were the first people to study fashion, in an attempt to understand the underlying causes for changes in style. In 1899 Theodore Veblen published *The Theory of the Leisure Class,* in which he explained fashion as a competition in which

Cravats

Dandies wore elaborate cravats, large squares of starched muslin that were folded into bands and wrapped around the neck to be tied at the front. These were so full and high that they made it impossible for wearers to lower their heads, giving the impression that they felt superior to everybody else. An 1828 book, *The Art of Tying the Cravat*, gave advice on the best knots or bows to use. It might take an hour or more to arrange the cravat every morning.

rich people tried to outdo each other by displaying their wealth. The best way to show off wealth, wrote Veblen, was to wear clothes which were obviously expensive and could only be worn for a short time before they had to be replaced by a new fashion. Impractical clothes, such as tight corsets, were also perfect, for they showed that the wearer did not have to work for a living.

The fashionable woman mocked in this 1825 cartoon has just learned that she has dropped her bustle, a layered undergarment worn to puff out her skirt at the back.

Women's Fashions

A middle- or upper-class Victorian woman was not expected to do any work, for she had servants to do everything for her. Her role was to be the "chief ornament" of her husband or of her father's household. According to the journal *The Saturday Review,* "It is the woman's business to charm and attract and to be kept from anything that may spoil the bloom of her character and tastes."

Modest Clothing

The ideal woman of the 1840s was supposed to be quiet, modest, and shy. Modesty was reflected in clothing styles. Dresses worn in the daytime, which had previously revealed a woman's shoulders, now covered her whole body, from the neck to the feet. Shoulders were only revealed by evening dresses worn at balls and dinner parties. Wide hats, worn until the late 1830s, went out of fashion, giving way to narrow bonnets, tied under the chin, which covered the sides of a woman's face.

It was fashionable to look small like Queen Victoria, who was five feet (1.52 m) tall, so women wore flat shoes, like slippers. The new dress shapes also made women look smaller, with tight sleeves, drooping shoulders, and long, narrow waists. Skirts were full and heavy, touching the floor, so that only the toes of a woman's shoes were ever seen. The preferred colors of the 1840s were modest dark greens and browns.

Corsets

Beneath her dress, a woman wore several layers of petticoats and a tightly laced corset, stiffened with strips of whalebone, which stretched from her chest down to her hips. This was thought to be medically beneficial, helping to support a woman's weak body. A tightly laced corset was also considered a sign of a good character. A "loose woman" was one who behaved in an immoral way.

Tight corsets affected the way that women moved. According to *The Handbook of the Toilet,* published in 1841, "The gait of an English-woman is generally stiff and awkward, there being no bend or elasticity of the body."

The women in this French engraving wear the modest fashions of the period, including bonnets which hide their faces.

A woman of the 1840s in an evening dress, revealing her neck and part of her shoulders.

Tight lacing made breathing difficult and led to fainting fits. Such fits were fashionable, for they demonstrated that a woman was delicate and needed to be looked after. *The Girls' Book of Diversions,* published in the 1840s, offered advice on how to faint: "the modes of fainting should all be as different as possible and may be very diverting." Women carried small bottles of "smelling salts" suspended from the waist of their dresses by chains. If they felt dizzy they would sniff their smelling salts, and when another woman fainted they would revive her by holding the bottle under her nose.

Jewelry

In the 1820s, women wore masses of jewelry with their evening dresses, including earrings, necklaces, gold chains with lockets, bracelets, and armlets. By the 1840s, such display had come to be seen as vulgar and showy. The modest woman of the 1840s often wore no more jewelry than a pair of bracelets and a chain for her bottle of smelling salts.

These decorative bottles once held "smelling salts"—a mixture of ammonia and perfume, which irritated the nose and lungs to stimulate breathing.

Cosmetics

In the early 1800s, women wore rouge makeup on their lips and cheeks to make themselves look healthy and lively. Respectable women stopped wearing rouge in the 1830s, preferring to look delicate and even sickly. The aim was to have what Victorian novels described as an "interesting pallor." Many drank vinegar, believing that this would give them pale skin. Victorian cosmetics were mostly lotions designed to hide freckles, and white face powders, used sparingly.

Clothes for Men

16e Octobre 1844.　　　　　　　700.

As women's clothes were growing more impractical to wear, men's fashions went in the opposite direction. In the 1840s, men gave up wearing jackets with tiny waists and padded shoulders. Bright colors and stripes were replaced by dark blues, browns, and blacks. The high cravat, which took so long to put on, disappeared, replaced by a ready-made neckpiece, called a stock, or ties with simple bows. There was much less variety of headwear, as men took to wearing top hats made of felt and silk.

The Middle Classes

This change in fashion reflected a larger change in society. The early nineteenth century saw the rise of the middle classes—the group who ranked higher in society than the working classes, who worked with their hands, yet were lower than the upper classes, who inherited their wealth and did not have to work at all. The middle classes included men from a wide range of professions, including factory owners, bankers, merchants, engineers, architects, civil servants, teachers, business managers, and office workers. What they all shared was a belief in hard work, and a desire to be seen as respectable gentlemen. They did not want to stand out from other men by wearing striking clothes, which they saw as ungentlemanly. They also wanted clothes that were easy to put on, for they were too busy to spend half their mornings tying cravats or being strapped into corsets.

Canes and Umbrellas

One of the signs of an eighteenth-century gentleman was that he had the right to carry a sword. Although swords went out of fashion in the 1770s, gentlemen found a new accessory in the form of a walking stick or cane made of polished wood, such as black ebony, topped with a golden or silver knob. Long umbrellas were also carried by fashionable men, who used them like walking sticks.

In the eighteenth century, both men and women had displayed their wealth with expensive, colorful embroidered fabrics, lace trimmings, jewelry, and impractical clothing such as high heels and wigs. The Victorian middle-class man left it to his wife or daughters to show off his wealth with expensive dresses, while he pursued the business of making money.

Conservative Attitudes

Although men's fashions continued to change, such changes took place much more slowly than the shifts in women's fashions. Developments were usually of minor features, such as the size of a jacket lapel or the shape of a top hat. In clothing, most Victorian men were conservative, meaning that they resisted change. They wanted a simple set of rules to follow about the correct clothes to wear for different occasions, such as going to work or calling on friends for tea. These were provided for them by books of etiquette (rules of polite behavior).

The middle classes admired the upper classes and followed their lead in fashions. Many of their attitudes were shared by the British royal family, for Queen Victoria and her husband, Prince Albert, were also conservative and serious-minded people who believed in the value of hard work and who distrusted flashy dressers.

The British taste in simple, dark clothing for men was imitated across Europe and in the United States.

A fashionable young man of the 1840s, wearing a frock coat and a top hat.

One reason for this was that the best men's tailors were said to be Englishmen, who had a long tradition of making well-cut clothes from woolen cloth.

Hairstyles

This 1844 portrait of a German princess shows the flat hairstyle of the period. As a child, her daughter wears her hair in a looser style.

A chair covered with an "antimacassar," to protect it from men's oily hair.

Women's Hair

Nineteenth-century women grew their hair long, only cutting it in times of serious illness, when short hair was supposed to aid recovery. As adults they never wore their hair down in public, but always pinned it up behind their heads. Until the 1860s, it was fashionable for women to have a center part, with their hair combed flat and drawn into a neat knot or bun behind. At first the knot was worn high at the back of the head, but in time it moved lower until, by the 1850s, it reached the neck. In the 1840s, there were fashions for long side ringlets and smooth loops worn over the ears.

Every evening, women let down their hair and combed it in front of a mirror, often saving the strands that fell out in a jar called a hair receiver. The saved hair was used to decorate lockets given to loved ones, and was even made into jewelry such as earrings, bracelets, and watch chains.

As women grew older, they usually kept the hairstyles of their youth. So in the 1860s, when young women were wearing elaborate hairstyles with artificial curls, the older ladies still had straight hair with center parts.

Men's Hair

Victorian men generally wore their hair short, with side or center parts. From the 1840s onward, they began to slick their hair down with perfumed Macassar oil, named after a region on the island of Celebes, where it was produced from seeds of tropical plants. Macassar oil was supposed to promote hair growth. To protect chairs from the greasy stains from hair oil, their tops were draped with cloth covers called antimacassars. In American speech this was eventually corrupted to "Auntie McCastor's."

In the early 1800s, all men shaved their chins. Beards had not been worn since the seventeenth century, and fashionable men wanted to look as youthful as possible. Only side whiskers and small moustaches, popular with army officers, were acceptable as facial hair. In the 1820s, the side whiskers grew longer until they met under the chin, forming a frame for the face. The first fashionable beard was a tiny tuft of hair under the chin, called a favorite.

Three examples of the wide variety of facial hairstyles worn by Victorian men.

Joseph Palmer

In the United States in 1830, a man called Joseph Palmer shocked the town of Fitchburg, Massachusetts, by growing a full beard. He was deeply religious, and grew his beard because they were worn in Biblical times. His appearance was regarded as so shocking that children threw stones at him in the street, and he was denounced in church by the local preacher. When a group of four men tried to shave him by force, Palmer defended himself with a knife, only to be arrested and charged with "an unprovoked assault." Palmer refused to pay the fine and was sent to Worcester prison for a year. He became famous across the nation as "the Bearded Prisoner of Worcester."

Joseph Palmer (see panel), who shocked America in the early 1830s with his beard, was ahead of his time. By the 1850s, many men were wearing full beards. In 1854 the *Westminster Review* described the beard as "identified with sternness, dignity, and strength ... the only becoming complement of true manliness." Even so, full beards were never popular with young men, who wanted to keep up with the latest fashions. Refusing to shave was a way of showing that a man had more important things to think about than fashion.

Bloomers and Crinolines

In the early 1850s, skirts grew wider with every year. The effect was achieved by wearing up to twelve layers of petticoats, including ones stiffened and padded with horsehair. Such clothes, both heavy and hot, were the most uncomfortable worn by women throughout the nineteenth century. People began to look for alternatives.

The "Bloomer" costume, promoted by Mrs. Amelia Bloomer in the early 1850s.

Bloomers

In 1851, Mrs. Amelia Jenks Bloomer, editor of a New York ladies' paper, *The Lily*, promoted a new costume for ladies combining a jacket and a light, knee-length skirt over baggy trousers, which were tight at the ankles. When she traveled to England to spread her ideas, Mrs. Bloomer was met with hostility and mockery. Women in "bloomers" were accused of "wearing the trousers," or trying to control their husbands. Only a few ladies attempted to wear bloomers, but soon gave them up. Writing in 1893, the early American feminist Lucy Stone recalled, "The bloomer costume was excellent.... When we undressed we felt no great sense of relief.... We could go upstairs without stepping on ourselves.... But useful as the bloomer was, the ridicule of the world killed it."

Crinoline

1856 saw the invention of a set of light steel hoops worn under the dress. This was called an artificial crinoline, originally the name of the stiffened petticoat, from *crin* (horsehair). The lightness of the garment was welcomed by women, and all classes quickly took to wearing crinolines. The earlier stiffened petticoats were forgotten, and the name *crinoline* now applied only to hoops. Even Mrs. Bloomer gave up her bloomers and dressed in crinolines.

By 1862 crinoline hoops accounted for a seventh of the weekly output of metal from Sheffield, center of the

British steel industry. In 1865 the journalist Henry Mayhew wrote, "Every woman now from the Empress on her Imperial throne down to the slavey in the scullery, wears crinoline, the very three year olds wear them.... At this moment ... men and boys are toiling in the bowels of the earth to obtain the ore of iron which fire and furnace and steam will ... convert into steel for petticoats."

Bigger Dresses

The effect on fashion of crinolines was to make dresses continue to increase in size, until they were six feet (1.8 m) wide. It became impossible for two women to go through a door at the same time. Men complained that they could no longer offer ladies their arm when walking with them. Women had to be careful in windy weather, when their dresses might be blown into the air. There were also women who accidentally set fire to themselves when they walked too near a fireplace. The Irish writer Oscar Wilde had two half sisters who burnt to death at a party in this way, the one trying to save the other who had caught on fire.

Crinolines, which also allowed shorter corsets to be worn, gave women a new sense of freedom. Many rebelled against the early Victorian idea that women should be modest, serious, and quiet. In an 1866 essay in *The Saturday Review,* Eliza Lynn Linton complained of modern women whose "sole idea of life is

plenty of fun." She wrote, "No one can say of the modern English girl that she is tender, loving, retiring or domestic.... All we can do is wait patiently until the national madness has passed and our women have come back to the old English ideal."

Ankle Boots

The crinoline, which exposed the feet and ankles, resulted in a new fashion for heeled ankle boots, laced halfway up the calf, replacing the earlier flat slippers. A shorter crinoline, the crinolinette, followed, to display the boots properly.

As this 1864 advertisement shows, there were many kinds of crinoline, including some whose steel bands were covered with horsehair-stuffed padding.

OUR MUTUAL FRIEND ADVERTISER.

SANSFLECTUM CRINOLINES.

Puffed Horse-hair Jupon
(*Registered*).

25s., 30s., and 33s. 6d.

F* Admirably adapted for the Promenade, having a decided train.' — *English-woman's Domestic Maga-zine.*

An amusing work on Crinoline gratis and post-free.

The Patent Ondina or Waved Jupon.

18s. 6d., 21s., and 26s. 6d.

'Allows the dress to fall in graceful folds.'— *Morning Post.*

Illustrations of Jupons gratis and post-free.

THE EFFECT OF PHILPOTT'S SANSFLECTUM CRINOLINES.

E. PHILPOTT,
Family Draper and Jupon Manufacturer, Wholesale and Retail,
37 *PICCADILLY, W.*

Chapter 2: The Clothing Industry

By the middle of the nineteenth century, people around the world were wearing fabrics produced in British factories. Different areas specialized in different textiles. Woolen cloth was manufactured in West Yorkshire, while Cheshire produced silk. The biggest industry of all was cotton manufacture, based in Lancashire, where it was said that "cotton was king." Lancashire cotton masters boasted that they supplied the home market before breakfast and the rest of the world afterward.

A West Indian cotton plantation of the 1820s, where black slaves pick and process cotton, under the eye of a white overseer.

Cotton: From Plant to Shirt

Cotton plants need a hot, dry climate to thrive. Five-sixths of the cotton manufactured in Britain came from the southern states of the United States, with the remainder coming mostly from India and Egypt, both part of the British Empire.

Plantations

Until the 1860s, American cotton plants were tended by black slaves working on large plantations. They planted the cotton in the spring and weeded the fields through the summer. In August the pods burst open, revealing seeds enclosed in white fluffy balls. These were picked by hand and then passed through a toothed machine called a gin, which separated the cotton from the seeds. It was then packed into bales to be shipped to the mills of Lancashire. Five million bales of cotton a year were shipped abroad from the United States.

In 1865, the American slaves were freed, but their working lives did not change greatly. The landowners invented a new system, called share cropping. Freed slaves continued to work in the fields in return for a share of the crop they produced. The planters still owned the land and the shops where the workers had to spend their earnings. At the end of a year, it was common for a sharecropper to be in debt to the landowner.

Factories

In the Lancashire factories the cotton went through several processes. It was passed through a carding machine whose teeth straightened the tiny fibers. The fibers were then drawn out, twisted, spun into thread, and woven into cloth on a loom. Cotton mills were hot and stuffy places to work, for the process required warm, still air. In the 1830s, the working day lasted from twelve to sixteen hours.

Child Labor

Factory work required little physical strength, and so children and teenagers, who could be paid less than adults, supplied a large part of the labor force. In 1844 William Cooke Taylor, author of *Factories and the Factory System*, wrote, "We would rather see boys and girls earning the means of support in the mill than starving by the road-side." Yet there was a longstanding campaign against the use of child labor, which was gradually limited by the British government. Between 1833 and 1891, the minimum age for factory workers was raised from nine to eleven years of age.

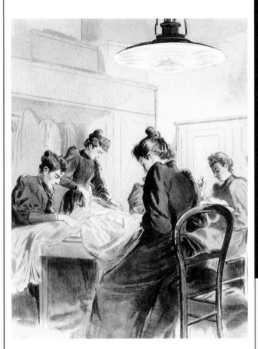

Seamstresses sewing dresses in a French workshop of the 1890s, under an electric lamp, a late Victorian invention.

Sweated Labor

Making clothes such as cotton shirts was usually a "sweated" trade, meaning that the employer paid workers for the number of pieces, or shirts, they completed rather than the hours they worked. The piece rate was so low that workers, often women, had to work long hours to make enough money to survive. In 1849 the journalist Henry Mayhew interviewed a woman who made shirts for a living. She said, "The collars, wristbands, and shoulder-straps are all stitched, and there are seven buttonholes in each shirt. It takes full five hours to do one.... I often work in the summer time from four in the morning to nine or ten at night—as long as I can see."

Beavers and Whales

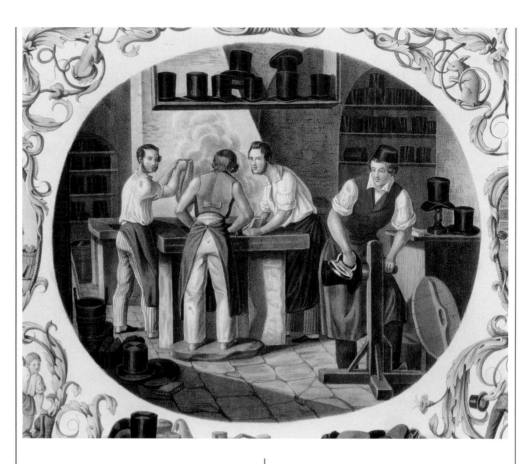

Two wild animals played a major role in the Victorian clothing industry. These were the North American beaver, whose dense fur was used to make hats, and the baleen whale, whose bony mouth plates were used to line corsets and make umbrella ribs. As a result of the Victorian demand for these products, both of these animals were driven to the edge of extinction.

Beavers

Since the Middle Ages, Europeans had made hats from beaver fur, scraping away the long outer hairs to reveal the thick wool underneath. Using steam and irons, this was shaped by hatters to make hard-wearing waterproof felt hats, with a silky sheen. As a result of the hat industry, beavers had disappeared from western Europe by the sixteenth century. In the seventeenth century, a rich new source of beavers was found in North America. Much of the exploration of the continent was carried out by beaver-fur trading companies, such as the Hudson's Bay Company. By the 1830s, beavers could only be found in the far north and west.

Hat City

One of the biggest centers of hat production was the city of Danbury, Connecticut, known as the Hat City. The number of hats produced each year in Danbury rose from one and a half million, in 1860, to five million in 1890. Although the industry has now disappeared, large amounts of mercury, used in hat production, still pollute the soil where the hatmakers' factories once stood.

Baleen

Baleen whales are animals with long plates of horny material, called baleen, which hang down from their upper jaws. These resemble giant, hairy combs which the animals use like a net, to trap food from the sea. Springy and tough, baleen was the perfect material to line corsets. The American whaling harbors of Bridgeport and New Haven, in Connecticut, were also centers of corset manufacture, where the garments were made by hand in factories and workshops.

By the 1860s, the slower types of baleen whale—bowheads and right whales—had been almost wiped out by hunters, who chased them in rowing boats with handheld harpoons. The whalers now turned their attention to other species of baleen whales, called rorquals, which swam too quickly to be caught by rowing boats. In the 1860s, whalers began to use fast, steam-powered "catcher boats," from which they fired harpoons with exploding shells.

Between 1870 and 1901, the value of baleen increased sixfold. Other whale products were no longer needed, for whale oil—previously used for lamps—had been replaced by kerosene, a product of petroleum. Whalers were now ripping out the baleen and throwing the rest of the animal back into the sea.

Mad Hatters

As beavers became scarcer, hatmakers were forced to use cheaper materials, particularly rabbit furs. In order to turn this into felt, it had to be coated with a solution of mercury, which roughened the fibers, helping them mat together. To shape the felt, it was boiled, dried, and then steamed. This led to hatters breathing in mercury fumes, which are highly poisonous. Many hatters ended up suffering from mercury poisoning, the symptoms of which included muscle twitching, a lurching walk, mental confusion, and slurred speech. This is the origin of the Victorian expression, "as mad as a hatter."

Lewis Carroll's 1865 children's book, *Alice in Wonderland,* includes a "Mad Hatter." He wears one of the top hats from his own shop, its price tag left in place.

The Sewing Machine

In the first half of the nineteenth century, dozens of inventors in the United States and Europe were trying to invent a sewing machine. There were many problems with early machines, in which thread usually broke after a short time. The first effective machine was the work of three American inventors: Walter Hunt, Elias Howe, and Isaac Merrit Singer.

Rival Inventors

Walter Hunt was a brilliant inventor, whose most famous invention was the safety pin. In the 1830s, Hunt built a sewing machine that used thread from two different sources. A curved needle with an eye at its point passed one thread through a piece of cloth, making a loop on the other side. Then a shuttle passed a second thread through the loop, making a "lockstitch." Hunt lost interest in his invention, and did not bother to apply for a patent (an official document granting an inventor the sole right to make and sell his invention, for a limited period).

In 1846 Elias Howe patented a machine which operated in the same

Elias Howe claimed that the idea for his sewing machine came to him in a dream.

Singer's first sewing machine was powered by a handcrank, labelled "D" in this drawing. He went on to replace this with a foot treadle, leaving both hands free to move the cloth.

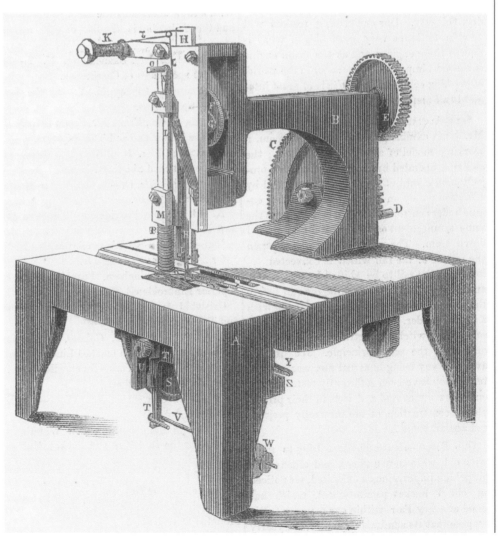

way as Hunt's, though he invented it independently. The machine was improved in 1851 by a third inventor, Isaac Merrit Singer, whose machine used a straight needle which moved up and down rather than from side to side, and which was powered by a foot crank rather than a handle. Unlike Howe's machine, which could only sew straight seams, a few inches at a time, Singer's could sew any type of seam continuously.

Singer's machines went into mass production in 1851. A better businessman than Hunt or Howe, Singer sold his machines, which were as expensive as cars are today, on installment credit plans. Housewives were able to pay for the machine in installments over a long period of time.

Howe accused Singer of stealing his ideas and sued him. Singer fought back, arguing that the lock-stitch had first been invented by Hunt, and he even paid Hunt to build a replica of his 1830s machine. Despite this, Howe won the case because Hunt had never applied for a patent. Singer was forced to pay Howe a share of his profits and, as a result, both Singer and Howe became millionaires.

Effects on Fashion

The sewing machine allowed clothes to be mass produced cheaply in factories. It also changed fashion, for it made it much easier to add decorative trimmings to dresses. In the 1870s, "Sylvia," the author of *How to Dress Well on a Shilling a Day* wrote, "We owe much of the over-

Clothes Factory

Although the sewing machine speeded up one part of clothes production, cloth still had to be cut by hand. Then, in 1860, John Barron, an English tailor, turned the woodworking band saw into a band knife, which could cut through several layers of cloth at one time. Barron's factory in Leeds, which used Singer sewing machines, was the first to mass produce ready-made clothes, including uniforms for railroad workers, the police force, and the British Army.

trimming now prevalent to the facilities offered by the sewing machines, which have become valued friends in many a household."

With its ornamental base, this 1899 sewing machine is a much more decorative object than the early Singer example on the opposite page. It is powered by a foot treadle.

New Colors

Until 1856, all clothes were colored with dyes made from natural products such as plants, minerals, insects, and shellfish. Purple, for example, was made from the murex shellfish, while red came from cochineal beetles. It required 17,000 beetles to make just one ounce (28 grams) of red dye, so natural dyes were often expensive to produce. Over time, the colors of naturally dyed clothes also faded, as a result of sunlight and washing.

William Perkin

In 1856 an eighteen-year-old English chemistry student named William Perkin was attempting to make artificial quinine, a drug to treat malaria. He was using aniline, a substance derived from coal tar. The experiment failed, leaving a dark, oily sludge. Perkin was about to throw it away when he decided to make a solution of it, and found that he had a bright purple liquid. On applying it to a piece of silk, he discovered that it worked as a dye.

Perkin had invented the first artificial dye, a bright purple, which he called mauveine. Unlike cloth dyed naturally, cloth colored with mauveine did not fade over time. Mauveine was also cheap to produce, for coal tar was an abundant waste product of gas manufacturing.

In 1857 Perkin opened a dyeworks on the Grand Union Canal in west London, and began to produce mauveine. The color first became fashionable in France, thanks to Empress Eugénie, who discovered that it matched her eyes. In 1858, after Queen Victoria wore a mauve dress to her daughter's wedding, there was an outbreak in England of what *Punch* magazine called "mauve measles." The novelist Charles Dickens wrote, "Oh, Mr. Perkin, thanks to thee for fishing out of the coal hole those precious stripes and bands of purple on summer gowns."

Meanwhile, Perkin was developing other artificial dyes, including

Perkin's new color, mauveine, is displayed in the dazzling stripes on the dress on the right.

Synthetic Perfume

While experimenting with coal tar, Perkin made another accidental discovery: a substance which smelled like new-mown hay, which he sold as a perfume. Chemists proceeded to use coal tar to make more artificial scents, including musk, violet, jasmine, and rose. Previously, the only way to make a perfume which smelled of roses was to use real rose petals. Perkin had invented the synthetic perfume industry.

A day dress of the 1850s.

Britannia Violet and Perkin's Green. The color of the canal water by his dyeworks was said to change from week to week, depending on which dye the company was producing. He now had competitors—French and German chemists who used anilene to produce Verguin's fuchsine (magenta), Martius yellow, bleu de Lyon, and aldehyde green. A race was on to make the brightest colors from coal tar.

The range of new colors was displayed at the London International Exhibition of 1862. The report by the exhibition judges described "a series of silks, cashmeres, ostrich plumes, and the like, dyed in a diversity of novel colors, allowed on all hands to be the most superb and brilliant that have ever delighted the human eye."

Until the 1860s, women dressed in a limited range of colors, chosen to go with each other in a pleasing way. The new aniline dyes led to women wearing outfits which combined several bright, contrasting colors. In 1872 a French visitor to London, Hippolyte Taine, complained, "the glare is terrible."

Paris Fashion

Early Victorian dressmakers were mostly women, who visited rich ladies at home to measure them and take orders for clothes. It was the customer, not the dressmaker, who chose the fabrics and the dress styles, from magazine illustrations. The dressmakers' work was seen as a craft rather than an art, and few of their names are remembered. The first famous dressmaker was an Englishman, Charles Frederick Worth (1825–95), who is called the father of "haute couture," or exclusive high fashion.

House of Worth

As a thirteen-year-old boy, Worth worked in a linen drapers, where he learned about fabric and trimmings. Fascinated by the history of fashion, he spent his spare time visiting art galleries to study dresses in old paintings. In 1846 he moved to Paris, where he began to work as a designer. In 1857 he opened his own business, Maison Worth (House of Worth), at 7 Rue de la Paix, Paris.

Worth was an expert designer, who saw himself as an artist, not a craftsman, and behaved as if he were doing women a favor by making clothes for them. Instead of visiting customers in their homes, they were expected to come to him. In order to make his business appear as exclusive as possible, Worth refused to serve ladies unless they had a letter of introduction from a previous customer.

It was an advantage to Worth that he was an Englishman in Paris. As a

Empress Eugénie

The one client whom Worth would serve in her home was Empress Eugénie (1826–1920), the beautiful Spanish wife of the French emperor Napoleon III. Eugénie spent vast sums on dresses and led rich women's fashions by her example, not just in France, but across the Western world.

Magazine illustrations, such as this 1880 example from *The Queen*, displayed the latest fashions from Maison Worth.

foreigner he stood outside the French class system and could behave in ways which would have seemed offensive coming from a Frenchman. The French writer Hippolyte Taine described what happened when a lady who had not been properly introduced tried to order a dress from Worth: "'Madame,' he said, 'By whom are you presented?' 'I don't understand.' 'I'm afraid you must be presented in order to be dressed by me.' She went away, suffocated with rage. But others stayed, saying, 'I don't care how rude he is so long as he dresses me.'"

The showrooms at Maison Worth included wooden mannequins modeling dresses, with mirrors carefully placed so that a customer would contrast her own inferior clothes with those on display. One room, thickly curtained to keep out the daylight, was lit by gas, so that a client could see how a dress might appear on her at a ball.

Worth pioneered methods used by couturiers today. He made his designs using patterns of linen or muslin, known as toile, which he draped over his client's body, adjusting them to make sure of a perfect fit. The toile patterns were then used to make the dress. Worth was also the first designer to make a seasonal collection of clothing rather than one-off garments.

Worth dressed the royal courts of Europe and attracted rich customers from as far away as Russia and the United States. In the capital cities of the United States and western Europe, other couturiers went into business. All of them followed the Paris fashions invented by Worth.

New Ways of Selling

The mass production of clothing required new ways of selling goods. The Victorian period saw the first shops offering ready-made clothes as well as the first department stores. People living far away from cities, in the American West, could now order their clothes from mail-order catalogs. The result was the birth of what is now called consumer culture. For the first time, shopping was seen as a leisure activity rather than a chore.

Every American farming family was said to own two books, the Bible and the Sears Roebuck mail-order catalog.

Department Stores

The first department stores to open, in the late 1840s and early 1850s, were A. T. Stewart's in New York, Bainbridges in Newcastle, and Bon Marché in Paris. For the first time, a customer could buy a complete outfit, including accessories, in a single store. Unlike earlier clothes stores, which usually kept goods locked away in glass cases, department stores displayed ready-made clothes in the open, encouraging browsers. Because department stores bought their goods in bulk, they could get better deals from their suppliers and charge cheaper prices. Customers also had the right to return goods and get a refund.

Window Shopping

The invention of a glass-pressing machine, in Boston in 1827, meant that large sheets of "plate glass" could be made. As a result, between 1830 and 1860, the size of the largest store window panes increased from seven by three feet (2 m by 1 m) to fourteen by eight feet (4 m by 2.4 m). These bigger windows allowed stores to display goods in new ways, to tempt passersby. In 1857 the English journalist George Augustus Sala described the windows of fashionable London stores as "museums of fashion in plate-glass cases." Describing the window dressers, he wrote, "By their nimble and practised hands the rich piled velvet mantles are displayed, the moire and glacé silks arranged in artful folds, the laces and gauzes, the

innumerable whim-whams and fribble-frabble of fashion, elaborately shown, and to their best advantage."

The Great Exhibition

In 1851, Britain held the "Great Exhibition of the Works of Industry of All Nations" in London, inviting manufacturers from around the world to display their finest goods. Between May and October, six million people visited the Great Exhibition, in the specially built Crystal Palace, which resembled a vast greenhouse of glass and iron. More than thirteen thousand exhibitors competed for prizes. The largest number went to the French, who were world leaders in fashion and design. This was just one of many Victorian exhibitions, which showed the public new fashions, and encouraged manufacturers to improve their products.

The novelist Charlotte Bronte, who visited the exhibition in June, wrote, "Whatever human industry has created you find there, from the great compartments filled with railroad engines and boilers ... to the glass covered and velvet spread stands loaded with the most gorgeous work of the goldsmith and silversmith."

This engraving shows the vast size of the Crystal Palace, which included 293,655 panes of glass in its construction.

Secondhand Clothes

The rich were always getting rid of unwanted clothes. When a jacket showed the slightest sign of wear, a gentleman would give it to his servants to dispose of. Ladies gave dresses that were no longer fashionable to their maids. The maids would have no opportunity to wear such clothes themselves, so they sold them to secondhand clothes dealers. All of the big cities of Europe and the United States had secondhand clothes dealers, often Jewish immigrants from eastern Europe.

A Shop in St. Giles

In 1877 the photographer John Thomson and the journalist Adolphe Smith published *Street Life in London,* the earliest collection of social documentary photographs. Thomson took a photograph of a secondhand clothes store in St. Giles, London. Describing the picture, Smith wrote, "The dealer whose portrait is before the reader cannot boast of a large business. She had been unfortunate in previous speculations, and illness had also crippled her resources, so that her stock is limited, and her purchasing power still more restricted."

Recycling

Old clothes were recycled by the dealers. If they could be cleaned and repaired, they went to a man called a clobberer. Adolphe Smith wrote that the clobberer "has cunning admixtures of ammonia and other chemicals, which remove the grease stains, he can sew with such skill that the rents and tears are concealed with remarkable success, and thus old garments are made to look quite new."

Upper-class fashions, such as dress coats, would not be worn by the poor. So they were cut up and made into new items of clothing by a man called a translator. He used the skirts of coats to make waistcoats or jackets for children. The rest of the cloth was often used to make caps.

A secondhand clothes store in London. Photography, a nineteenth century invention, provides a rich source of evidence for Victorian dress.

Stealing

The most common Victorian crime was stealing clothes, to be sold to the secondhand dealers. The London Victorian clothes dealers had a reputation as "fences," or receivers of stolen goods. In his novel *Oliver Twist*, Charles Dickens depicts a Victorian fence, Fagin, who trains a gang of child pickpockets to lift handkerchiefs from gentlemen's pockets.

The easiest way to steal clothes was to take items left to dry on the washing lines of laundries. Many of these operated in the outer suburbs of Victorian cities, away from the smoke of the center, where they cleaned the white shirts and petticoats of the middle and upper classes. Stealing clothes from washing lines was called "snowing." Thieves always found a ready market for good-quality linen and cotton among secondhand clothes dealers.

Many of these re-modeled garments were taken for sale to London's famous Petticoat Lane street market, which became a great clothing exchange. Here, a poor man could buy a cabinet minister's heavy overcoat; a poor bride a fine gown for her wedding.

When clothes were too worn out for the translator or clobberer, they were sold to wool manufacturers to be turned into new cloth. Old clothes from all over Europe ended up in the mills of Yorkshire where, according to Adolphe Smith, "They are torn into shreds by toothed wheels ... till they are reduced to the condition of wool. They may then be mixed with a certain amount of new wool, and finally reappear as new cloth, woven according to the latest pattern.... Thus the cloth of our newest coat is, after all, probably made from the cast-off garment of some street beggar!"

A young pickpocket runs off with a gentleman's pocket watch.

Chapter 3: The Stages of Life

Like people throughout history, the Victorians used clothes to mark the different stages of life, from a child's white christening robe to a bride's white dress and a widow's black veil. Growing up was marked by boys putting on long trousers, and girls wearing longer dresses and pinning their hair up.

Babies

Babies wore diapers of folded linen or cotton, which might be knotted or fastened with a safety pin, after this was invented in 1849. Infants of both sexes wore long, white dresses, often trimmed with lace. Once a baby was old enough to crawl, the dress was shortened to ankle length. When they were taken out for a walk in a "perambulator" (baby carriage), babies wore elaborate bonnets.

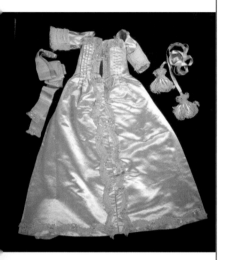

A baby's christening robe, made of shiny satin.

Boys

Boys continued to wear dresses, and have their hair long, after they learned to walk. Between the ages of three and seven, depending on their mother's wishes, they would have their hair cut short and be "breeched," or put into trousers.

The skeleton suit, worn from the 1790s until the 1830s, was the first outfit specifically designed for children to wear. Previously, children had worn scaled-down versions of adult clothes. Its name came from its close-fitting style, said to make boys look as thin as skeletons. The outfit was described by Charles Dickens in 1839 as "a contrivance for displaying ... a boy's figure by fastening him into a very tight jacket, with an ornamental row of buttons over each shoulder and then buttoning his trousers over it so as to give his legs the appearance of being hooked on just under his arm pits."

The most popular boy's outfit, worn from the 1840s until the early 1900s,

The "Little Lord Fauntleroy" suit, fashionable in the 1880s.

was the sailor suit. This originated in Britain, but then spread to the rest of Europe and the United States. It was originally worn for patriotic reasons. The British had the most powerful navy in the world, and boys loved to read about great naval heroes and battles.

In 1885 the American novelist Francis Hodgson Burnett published *Little Lord Fauntleroy*, whose boy hero is described as "a graceful, childish figure in a black velvet suit, with a lace collar, and with love locks waving about the handsome, manly little face." From the 1880s until around 1910, there was a craze for the "Little Lord Fauntleroy" costume, which was based on clothes worn in the seventeenth century. It was loved by mothers but detested by little boys.

Girls

The standard dress for a girl was a short skirt, with a blouse, jacket, and hat. Between the ages of four and sixteen, the hemline of a girl's skirt gradually lowered, until it reached the ankles. A sixteen-year-old girl was considered to be a young woman and showed her new status by pinning her hair up.

In 1935 the writer Eleanor Acland recalled that, as a girl in the 1880s, she had to wear six items of underwear: a woolen vest, drawers, a calico chemise, stockings, stays, and a petticoat. She wrote, "What I ... most envy the little girls of today is the fewness and simplicity of their garments."

Wedding Dresses

In the early nineteenth century, wedding dresses could be any color. For her wedding in 1840, Queen Victoria chose to wear a satin dress that was white, a color linked with purity, and set a fashion for all future brides. She also wore a veil with orange blossoms, which would become the favorite flower worn by Victorian brides, usually on their dresses.

In Mourning

On December 14, 1861, Prince Albert, husband of Queen Victoria, died of typhoid, leaving a forty-two-year-old widow and nine children. The royal family immediately dressed in black, the color of mourning. For the next eight years, the royal servants all wore black armbands. The queen would live on for another thirty-nine years, yet she would never again wear any color except black, white, or deep violet.

High Mortality

The Victorian period was a time of high mortality, even among the upper classes. The death of children, in particular, was a common event, caused by diseases such as cholera, typhoid, diphtheria, influenza, measles, and chicken pox. In 1899, in the wealthiest part of Liverpool, 136 babies in every thousand died before they reached the age of one. So most families had to wear mourning clothes at some time or another.

Rules for Mourning

Upper- and middle-class Victorians followed strict rules about the clothes they wore following a death in the family. The period of mourning depended on the family relationship. It ranged from two and a half years, for a widow grieving for a husband, to six weeks—the time mothers mourned the parents-in-law of their married children.

The rules were simple for men, who wore a black armband over an ordinary black suit. It was more complicated for women, who had to wear different clothes at four different stages of mourning. During "first," or "deep," mourning, widows wore a plain black dress covered with crepe, a dull, crinkled black silk. When they went out, they hid their faces beneath a black veil. After a year and a day, widows moved on to "second mourning," when the crepe

Jet Jewelry

Jet is a black stone made from fossilized monkey puzzle trees. With its soft texture and high polish, it was the ideal material for mourning jewelry. The best jet was found in Whitby in Yorkshire, where it was mined from cliffs or collected from beaches. In 1873 two hundred Whitby men worked as jet miners, while a further 1,500 men and boys were employed in making mourning jewelry.

on their dresses was limited to decorative trimmings and they could now wear the veil back, revealing their faces. After a further nine months, they reached the third stage, "ordinary mourning," when they stopped wearing crepe, replacing it with shiny black silk, trimmed with ribbons and jet. The last stage, "half mourning," lasted for six months or more, when they could wear soft colors such as lilac and gray.

By wearing mourning for thirty-nine years, Queen Victoria was acting in an unconventional way. In 1862 she even wore black to her second daughter's wedding, although widows were expected to wear half-mourning colors at weddings so that they would not spread gloom. As the queen, she could exhibit behavior which would have been criticized in commoners.

Observing the rules correctly was extremely expensive. Fashions in mourning dresses changed just as quickly as those in everyday clothes, and so women could not save their mourning dresses for the next death in the family. It was said to be unlucky to keep crepe in the house after the mourning period ended. So the dresses were always sold to secondhand clothes dealers.

This portrait shows Queen Victoria in 1887, still dressed in half mourning for her husband Albert, who had died twenty-six years earlier. The blue sash is the emblem of the Order of the Garter.

Chapter 4: Occasional Clothes

A striking feature of the Victorian period was the number of times each day that upper- and middle-class people changed their clothes. Different dresses and coats were worn in the daytime and in the evening, and there were also particular outfits for different activities, such as horse riding or playing tennis.

A gentleman in a dressing gown.

Dishabille

Unlike women, who dressed formally throughout the day, men could wear comfortable clothes, called dishabille (undress) at breakfast or when relaxing in the evening. Over trousers and a shirt, they would wear a richly colored dressing gown and a round embroidered cap, often with a tassel. In the 1870s, there was a fashion for breakfast jackets, which were blue or maroon velvet with quilted satin lapels. The next decade saw the coming of smoking jackets, which were velvet with cord edging.

Morning and Evening Dresses

Women wore a morning dress in the daytime, changing into an evening dress for dinner. There was a wide variety of styles for both types of clothes. The main difference was that morning dresses were less richly decorated, and covered a woman's shoulders.

According to *The Habits of Good Society* (1855), "There are four kinds of coat which a well dressed man must have; a morning coat, a frock-coat, a dress-coat, and an overcoat." The frock coat was a jacket with a long, square front, while the morning coat had swallowtails. Both came in a variety of colors and were worn during the daytime. In the evening, men dressed for dinner, switching to formal evening dress, consisting of black trousers and a tailcoat, a low black or white waistcoat, a starched white shirtfront, and a white bow tie.

Hats

Everybody wore hats outdoors, and formal male dress required a black, silk top hat. This was raised, on greeting a lady, or simply touched when meeting another gentleman. Failure to greet someone, called "cutting" them, was a terrible insult. There were books of etiquette

Bedtime

Women wore a long nightgown in bed, and both men and women often wore white nightcaps to sleep in. Men slept in long nightshirts until the 1880s, when they started to wear pajamas, a fashion brought over from India by returning British soldiers and civil servants. The Hindi word *pajama* means "leg clothing," referring to the light trousers worn by both Indian men and women as day wear. Pajamas came in various colors and were often striped.

explaining the right time to take a hat off when visiting someone. Gentlemen did not leave their hats in the hall, but carried them into the drawing room to greet the hostess, where they left them on a table or a chair. According to an American book, *Martine's Handbook* (1866), "a gentleman never sits in the house with his hat on in the presence of ladies for a single moment. Indeed, so strong is the force of habit that a gentleman will quite unconsciously remove his hat on entering a parlor, or drawing room, even if there is no one present but himself."

Wearing the wrong clothes for the wrong occasions was almost as shocking as wearing no clothes at all. In 1899, *The Tailoring World* declared,

"Formerly no man in full rig [formal dress] would have walked down Piccadilly with a man in a round hat and short coat; and a lady on meeting the latter would have pretended she did not recognize him."

A lightweight overcoat, or top coat, worn by gentlemen during the daytime.

This pink satin evening dress was designed by Charles Frederick Worth. It is richly decorated with bead embroidery.

Leisure Wear

A game of mixed doubles. Victorian women wore long dresses to play tennis.

A striped blazer and straw hat was worn for boating—rowing on a lake or river.

Upper- and middle-class Victorians enjoyed many different sporting and leisure activities, including riding, hunting, fishing, boating, cricket, golf, tennis, croquet, archery, ice-skating, and hill walking. Different leisure activities demanded different sets of clothing. In 1884 *The Gentleman's Fashion Magazine* pronounced, "Every man with a grain of respectability, on the river puts on white trousers, with white flannel shirt, straw hat, striped flannel coat."

Hunting

There were various hunting outfits, depending on the sport. For foxhunting on horseback, men and women wore bright scarlet jackets which were called hunting pink. The name derived from the tailor Thomas Pink, a popular maker of hunting coats in the late eighteenth century. Stalking and shooting deer in the Scottish highlands called for subdued colors, so that the hunter would blend into the surroundings and not startle the animals. Men wore thick woolen socks, brown jackets, and knee-breeches made of tweed, a hard-wearing wool fabric with a diagonal weave. There was also a tweed "deerstalker" hat, with ear protectors, which could be tied up on top. This is the hat associated with the famous Victorian fictional detective, Sherlock Holmes.

Boating

For cricket and boating, men wore white flannel trousers and shirts beneath a bright jacket, often with colorful stripes, called a blazer. This is thought to have originated with the St. Margaret Boat Club in Cambridge University, whose members wore a red striped jacket which was said to "blaze" on the water. In the late Victorian period, the blazer was adopted as school uniform for boys and girls. A columnist in *The Ladies' World* of 1887 wrote, "The striped flannel jackets, under the familiar name 'blazer' brilliant in coloring, created for the river and the cricket field are worn on nearly all occasions now by girls and boys."

Croquet, Archery, and Tennis

The most popular sports for wealthy women were croquet, tennis, and archery. Women wore hats, gloves, and long dresses, which were not very different from their usual daywear, and just as impractical. One reason why croquet was so popular with women was that it required little physical effort, and could be played while wearing a tight corset.

Mountaineering

In the 1850s, adventurous Englishmen took to mountaineering as a sport, forming climbing clubs, and scaling peaks in Wales and the Swiss Alps. Mountain climbers wore similar clothes to those used in deerstalking, with thick jackets and knee breeches made of tweed or whipcord, another tough material. The jackets and trousers were waterproofed by painting them with a paste made of soap and boiled linseed oil. Boots were given hobnail soles, to make them grip the mountainside.

Seaside

Until the nineteenth century, the British seaside was not considered a holiday location. However, smoky Victorian cities made fresh sea air

Bathing Costumes

Victorian bathing costumes were made of thick serge and covered as much of the body as possible. For women this meant a body stocking beneath a short skirt, often striped. It did not matter that such clothes were hard to swim in, for women usually wore them only for wading. Few people learned how to swim properly until the twentieth century. Wearing a bathing costume was a great relief from the usual corset and layers of clothing.

Women in heavy bathing costumes, wading up to their necks in the sea.

attractive, and the railroads placed the coast within reach of everyone. Even the working classes could go to the sea for day trips from the big factory towns. Suntans were not fashionable, for they were associated with country people, who had to work outdoors. To protect their white skin, ladies carried parasols and wore wide straw hats, while men wore straw boaters.

Chapter 5: Working Clothes

At the market: a fishseller (left) and a baker (right)

A Danish newspaper seller, whose cart is being loaded, wears a short light jacket and a peaked cap.

The commonest sight in any Victorian town was of men in black suits. This was like a uniform, worn by businessmen, bank managers, store assistants, railroad station masters, teachers, civil servants, and the many thousands of office clerks. The black suit was an ideal garment for wearing every day in a town where the air was smoky from coal fires. Its color also suggested that the wearer was serious and trustworthy. The dark suit, still worn in offices around the world today, is one legacy of the Victorian era.

Butchers and Fish Dealers

In certain trades, men wore distinctive costumes, which allowed them to be recognized, and which were often worn with pride. In Britain, the best butchers wore blue coats, a custom going back to the seventeenth century. They also had aprons with horizontal stripes, while fish dealers wore aprons with vertical stripes.

Such clothes inspired trust in the customers, who needed to know that the meat and fish they bought was fresh. In 1867 the writer James Greenwood contrasted a butcher serving his middle-class readers with another in a slum district: "Your butcher wears a hat, generally a genteel hat, and a blue coat, and a respectable apron; perhaps, even snowy sleeves and shiny boots.... Contrasted with him the butcher of Squalors' Market ... wears on his head a cap made of the hairy hide of the bison or some other savage beast; his red arms are bare to the elbows, and he roars continuously."

Skilled craftsmen, and most storekeepers, wore white aprons, which were sent to the laundry to be cleaned. Like the butcher's blue coat, a gleaming white apron was said to inspire pride in the wearer and confidence in his customers. People in less skilled jobs, such as knife sharpeners and market sellers, wore cheap aprons made from brown sacking.

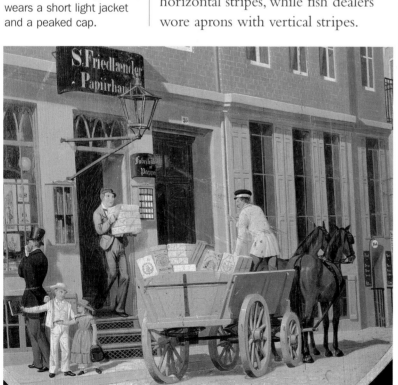

Practical Clothes

Some work required clothing designed for practical reasons. Market porters, who carried piles of boxes and baskets on their heads, wore hats with large leather pads. Sewer workers wore long leather boots that rose above the knees and that were covered with grease to protect them from the water.

In every town there were coal sellers, who delivered coal to houses, and dustmen, who collected the ash from fires. Both wore knee-breeches with short smock frocks, and hats with a wide, fan-shaped neck-piece at the back, like the sou'wester worn by fishermen. The journalist Henry Mayhew wrote that you could tell dustmen from coalmen at a glance, for "the latter are invariably black from coal dust, while the dustmen, on the contrary, are gray with ashes."

The dirtiest workers of all were the chimney sweeps, who spent most of their lives coated in soot. Even though they wore black suits and top hats, they were seen as the lowest order of workers and were looked down on by almost everybody else. According to Mayhew, "The peculiar nature of their work giving them not only a filthy appearance, but an offensive smell (forces) them to herd together apart from others."

At the market: a barrow woman and a shrimp seller, carrying her net.

Men in typical working clothes buy shellfish from a market stall.

Paper Hats

Carpenters, stone masons, painters, glassblowers, and plumbers wore box-shaped hats made from a large square of folded paper. This hat served no practical purpose, but was worn as a sign that the wearer belonged to a skilled trade. It showed that he knew how to fold the paper correctly to make one.

Uniforms

The word *uniform* means "with no variations." People in uniform are those who dress alike, such as soldiers, policemen, firemen, prisoners, and nurses. The Victorian period saw an increase in the number of uniforms, which gave the Victorians a sense of order in a world which was going through rapid and bewildering changes.

A policeman's uniform included his individual number; in this case "345." This allowed members of the public to identify an officer if they wished to make a complaint about him.

Police

The modern police originated in Britain in 1829, when Sir Robert Peel founded the London Metropolitan Police Force, the first full-time professional police force in the world. The "peelers," as they were known were so effective that other forces were set up throughout Britain and abroad. In 1845 New York established its own police force modeled on the British one.

The purpose of a police uniform is to allow a member of the public to recognize an officer. Early uniforms were carefully designed to win public support for the police. Officers wore dark blue coats with shiny brass buttons, like clothes worn by servants. This was to show that the policeman was there to serve the public. Police uniforms were unlike those worn by soldiers, who were feared by the public for the violence with which they broke up riots and demonstrations.

The first policemen wore top hats. This was a sign of respectability which made a policeman stand out in working-class areas where nobody else wore them. By making an officer look taller, the hat was supposed to give him greater authority. The

Judges and Wigs

British judges wore white horsehair wigs and long red and white gowns, clothing which dates back to the seventeenth century. The purpose of this deliberately old-fashioned dress was to make the judge appear as a representative of a long legal tradition. Wigs were thought to give a judge a dignified and solemn appearance.

problem with top hats was that they gave no protection in a fight, and were easy to knock off with a stone or a brick. Knocking policemen's hats off was a popular sport in some districts. As a result, in 1864, in Britain the top hat gave way to a tall helmet.

In the United States, the first policemen refused to wear uniforms, apart from a badge. They did not wish to look like "liveried lackeys" (servants), a term they used to describe British policemen. It was only in 1853 that the New York city police adopted a blue frock coat with brass buttons, and a peaked cap, replaced by a tall helmet in the 1880s.

Prisoners

When convicted prisoners entered a Victorian prison, the first thing they had to do was to surrender their clothes and put on a prison uniform. This included a badge with a number, which would be the prisoner's name while serving the sentence. Like giving up personal clothes, losing their names meant that they had lost their individual identities. This was part of the punishment. In some prisons, convicts even had to wear masks when exercising to prevent them from getting to know each other. Other prisoners were thought to be a bad influence.

After putting on their uniforms, prisoners had their hair cut short, and male prisoners had their beards and moustaches shaved off. Florence

Maybrick spent fifteen years in prison for poisoning her husband, though she claimed she was innocent. She described the prison haircut in her autobiography: "The warder ... stepped quickly forward, and with a pair of scissors cut off my hair to the nape of my neck. This act seemed, above all others, to bring me to a sense of my degradation [low state], my utter helplessness."

Uniforms worn by men and women in the prisons of London in the 1840s.

Military Uniforms

Military uniforms were invented by the ancient Romans, whose soldiers wore identical armor over short red tunics. This encouraged the men to think of themselves as members of a group rather than as individuals, making them better disciplined, and more effective fighters. Uniforms also allowed them to tell a friend from an enemy in the heat of a battle. Nineteenth-century uniforms served the same purpose. In the early 1800s, armies still went into battle in bright colors. British soldiers fighting the French at Waterloo, in 1815, wore scarlet coatees (short jackets) and tall bearskin hats, to make themselves look more imposing.

Tight Clothes

Waterloo was followed by a long period of peace in Europe, when uniforms became stiffer and tighter. Such clothes were designed for the parade ground rather than the battlefield. The difficulty of fighting in tight clothes, which restricted movement and made it hard to breathe, was revealed during the Crimean War of 1854. The British

Uniforms were worn to display rank, with the most elaborate dress worn by the senior officers, as shown in this illustration of men and boys in the British Navy.

army then adopted a loose tunic, which covered the hips and offered more protection.

Blue against Gray

In 1861 a civil war broke out in the United States between the southern states, or Confederacy, and the northern states, or the Union. Each side had to quickly raise armies and supply uniforms. At first, all sorts of strange uniforms were adopted, including Highland kilts and brightly colored baggy trousers. Eventually, the Union clothed its soldiers in blue, while the Confederacy chose gray.

Although Wisconsin was part of the Union, its soldiers wore gray at the start of the war. The disadvantage of

Rifles

A great change to uniforms was made necessary in the 1850s, with the introduction of mass-produced muskets which were rifled. Unlike earlier muskets, which had smooth barrels, rifles had spiral grooves carved inside them, which made a bullet spin as it flew through the air, increasing its accuracy. A rifle was deadly at three hundred yards (274 m), triple the range of a musket. For a marksman armed with a rifle, a soldier in a scarlet tunic made an excellent target. Soldiers would now have to wear uniforms which helped them to blend in with their surroundings rather than stand out.

this was shown at the first big battle of the war, at Manassas, in July 1861, when the Wisconsin soldiers found themselves being shot at by both sides. After the battle they were reissued with blue uniforms.

Scarlet against Brown

The shortcomings of scarlet were made clear in 1880–1, when Britain fought a war against the Boers, Dutch settlers in South Africa. In February 1881, at the Battle of Majuba Hill, a force of scarlet-coated British soldiers was defeated by Boer marksmen, who found it easy to shoot at the men in their bright tunics. The Boers wore drab browns, which helped them to blend in with the dry African scenery.

After Majuba Hill, a government enquiry suggested the adoption of gray for battle dress. The Duke of Cambridge, army commander-in-chief, resisted the change. In 1883 he said, "I should be sorry to see the day when the English Army is no longer in red.... I think the soldier had better be taught not to hide himself, but to go gallantly to the front ... the man who does that has a much better chance of succeeding than the man who hides himself."

It was not until the late 1890s that the British army was given khaki (brown) uniforms for battlefield service. Khaki, originally adopted by the British army in India, comes from a Hindi word meaning "dusty colored."

A Confederate (top) and a Union soldier (bottom) during the American Civil War.

Servants

Servants formed one of the biggest groups in Victorian society, and more women worked as servants than in any other job. The number of servants employed in a single house ranged from fifty, in a great country house, down to a single "maid-of-all-work" in a lower-middle-class home.

In a great house the servants were organized in ranks. The most important were the housekeeper and the butler. The housekeeper was a middle-aged woman in charge of the accounts. She paid the bills and hired and fired most of the female servants. The butler was the head of the male staff and had responsibility for the household silver and the wine supplies. He wore black evening dress, similar to a gentleman's, though a butler's attire would usually include a visual clue, such as a striped waistcoat, to show guests at dinner parties that he was not one of them but a servant.

A footman in livery with white-powdered hair.

Footmen

Footmen were the servants who answered the front door, delivered letters, and waited at dinner. Their role was to display the wealth and taste of their employers to visitors. Footmen wore a uniform called livery, consisting of an eighteenth-century style coat, knee-breeches, and white stockings. They often wore wigs, or powdered their hair. John James, a footman in the 1890s, described the unpleasant daily task of powdering: "After the hair had been moistened, soap was put on and rubbed into a stiff lather, and the

Buttoning

During the Victorian period, clothes became standardized, with men's buttons on the right and women's on the left. It is thought that the reason for this was that rich ladies were dressed by their maids. Most people are right-handed and find it convenient to hold the button with their right hand. For men, who dressed themselves, the best place to have buttons was on the right side. This was reversed for ladies' maids, who faced the clothes they buttoned.

combing was done.... Powder was then applied with a puff and the wet mess allowed to dry on the head until it became quite firm."

The taller the footman, the more he could expect to earn, so you could judge the wealth of a rich family by the height of its footmen. A footman over six foot (1.8 m) tall could demand twice the salary of one who was only five feet six (1.7 m). Hippolyte Taine, a French visitor to England, was impressed by the size of the footmen: "They wear white cravats with large faultless bows, scarlet or canary-colored kneebreeches, are magnificent in shape and amplitude [fullness], their calves especially are enormous."

Lady's Maid

The lady's maid was the personal servant of the mistress of the house, brushing her hair at night, and helping her to dress in the morning. She had to look after her mistress's clothes, repairing them with a needle and thread and ensuring that they were cleaned and pressed. One advantage of her job was that she would usually be given the lady's cast-off clothing.

Housemaids

Most of the hard work in a house was done by housemaids. They made beds, carried coal, lit fires, cleaned fireplaces, laid tables, beat rugs, and scrubbed floors. A housemaid's uniform consisted of a dark dress, a white apron, and a tall white cap, which covered the hair. The state of the housemaid's white apron was a good guide to how clean she was, and therefore how good she was at her job.

Left: This woman is being tied into her dress by her "lady's maid," her personal servant.

A housemaid, dressed in apron and white cap, does the ironing.

Laborers

Here, German laborers lay a telegraph cable in a trench which they have dug. The man in charge can be identified by his more expensive bowler hat.

The Victorian era was a time of vast building programs, as railroads spread across Britain and factory towns grew, doubling in size every ten years. This expansion depended mainly on unskilled laborers, such as the "navvies" who tunneled through hillsides and laid railroad lines, and the miners who dug the coal out of the earth. Such laborers dressed for practical reasons, in tough fabrics that withstood the wear and tear of their work.

Navvies

In the mid 1840s, 200,000 men were building railroads in Britain. They were called navigators, shortened to navvies, a name originally given to eighteenth-century canal builders. A third of them were Irish, driven by poverty and a terrible famine to leave their homeland in search of work.

Navvies wore shirts made of calico, a coarse, light cotton named after Calcutta in India, where it was first made. Their jackets were made of a tough material called jean, a mixture of cotton and wool, named after Genoa in Italy. For trousers the men wore knee-breeches made of corduroy, a hard-wearing cotton fabric with raised ridges. This was invented in France in the late eighteenth century, and was first called the king's cord, perhaps because it was worn by royal servants. There were just two items of clothing which navvies wore for display rather than practical reasons: a patterned waistcoat, which might be red with black spots, and a brightly colored "neckerchief."

Coal Miners

Life in Victorian times depended on coal. Coal was the fuel which was burned in every fireplace and which drove the factory machines and train engines. Coal was also used to make gas for lighting, and at the end of the century it was burned in power stations to make electricity. Unlike other Victorian industries, coal mining was all done by hand, by men working deep underground in narrow tunnels, hacking at the coal face with picks. The men were often naked, for it was hot, and few clothes could stand up to crawling on hands and knees along a mine shaft, often through water. Women and children also worked in the mines, carrying coal, opening and closing ventilation doors, and "hurrying," or pulling and pushing the wheeled coal carts.

In 1842 the British government carried out an inquiry into coal mining that shocked the nation, for it revealed that women, wearing trousers, had to work with naked men. A seventeen-year-old hurrier, Patience Kershaw, told the enquiry, "I hurry in the clothes I have now got on—trousers and a ragged jacket.... I

Jeans

In California in the 1850s, gold prospectors began to wear trousers made of denim, named after Nimes in France. This was a cotton fabric with a diagonal weave, using threads of blue and white. Harder wearing than jean, it eventually replaced it in the United States as the favorite cloth for hard work, and the trousers made from this material would acquire the name "jeans," from the earlier material. Like the dark suit, denim jeans—now worn by all classes of society around the world—is another legacy of the Victorian era.

am the only girl in the pit; there are about twenty boys and fifteen men, all naked. I would rather work in mill than in coal-pit." As a result of the inquiry, a law was passed preventing the employment of women underground.

A navvy.

A collier.

Country Workers

Workers in the countryside were affected little by changing fashions. Across western Europe laborers wore traditional folk costumes that had not changed for centuries. There were strong regional variations in the colors and decorations used. In one area, all of the men might wear blue smocks, while in another the color would be light gray. In Britain, this regional variation declined as more men took to wearing the dark suits of townspeople.

Smock Frocks

The main garment worn in Britain by early-Victorian country laborers was the loose cotton smock frock, worn since the seventeenth century. The smock was worn over corduroy knee-breeches and gaiters (leather bands wrapped around the calves). A laborer would usually own two smocks: one for working in, and a best one to wear to church on Sunday. A smock frock was comfortable, hard wearing, and

These women are picking hops, used in brewing. Like many Victorian paintings, this presents an idealized view of life in the countryside.

practical. It kept out the wind, and it could be waterproofed with linseed oil. Looking back to the Victorian age in 1904, the garden designer Gertrude Jeckyll wrote, "No better thing has ever been devised for any outdoor wear.... It turns (repels) an astonishing amount of wet."

During the Victorian period, the spread of the railroads brought town and country together for the first time. Large numbers of country people moved to the growing towns to find work. At country fairs, people could now see salesmen and other townspeople wearing black suits. Those who could afford to wanted to imitate them.

There were different classes in the countryside, with tradesmen, wheelwrights, and blacksmiths looking down on farm laborers, who were the lowest-paid British workers. From the 1830s onward, men and boys from these upper ranks began to imitate townspeople, dressing in jackets and trousers made of a cheap fabric called shoddy. Shoddy was made by tearing apart older cloth and mixing it with new fibers. The word has come to mean anything poorly made or of inferior quality.

Joseph Arch (1826–1919), the son of a shepherd, was one of the few country people to write his autobiography, which he published in 1898. As a boy he wore a smock frock to school along with all of the other sons of farm laborers, while the sons of tradesmen and wheelwrights

wore coats of shoddy. Archer recalled, "These peacocky youngsters would cheek the lads in smock-frocks whenever they got the chance, and many a stand-up fight we used to have—regular pitched battles of smock-frock against cloth-coat, they were, in which smock-frock held his own right well."

From the 1860s onward, growing numbers of farm workers abandoned their smocks and gaiters for jackets and trousers, bought secondhand. Writing in 1884, the novelist Thomas Hardy described the changes he had seen in Dorset fairs: "A glance up the high street ... twenty or thirty years ago revealed a crowd whose general color was whitey-brown.... Now the crowd is as dark as a London crowd. The change is owing to the rage for cloth clothes which possesses the laborers of today."

A farm laborer wearing a smock, sharpens his scythe.

Countrywomen

Like men, countrywomen imitated the dress of townspeople. In Dorset, the younger women gave up wearing the traditional plain bonnet, cotton gown, and flat boots. They began to wear hats with beads and feathers, brightly dyed dresses, and boots with heels, like those of town ladies. Country folk preferred wearing such clothes, even though they were secondhand, to brand-new traditional clothes.

The Poorest of All

Hans Christian Anderson's story, *The Little Match Girl*, tells the sad tale of a poor girl who freezes to death on the street on New Years' Eve.

Every large Victorian city had slum districts, where the poor lived in crowded conditions, in badly built houses without proper drains or running water. Large numbers of the poor were homeless, sleeping in the streets. These people had no choice in the clothes they wore, and often dressed in rags.

The Victorian public was aware of the terrible suffering of the poor, which was described in the popular novels of Charles Dickens, and the work of the investigative journalist Henry Mayhew. Yet there were big disagreements about what, if anything, could be done about the situation. Many Victorians blamed the poor for their poverty, arguing that it was their laziness that was to blame.

In his book *London Labour and the London Poor* (1862), Mayhew described the Asylum for the Houseless Poor, an East London institution offering temporary shelter to the homeless when the temperature dropped below freezing point. There was room for three hundred people, though many more tried to gain admittance. Mayhew saw a crowd of five hundred waiting for the doors to be opened at five p.m. He described them "shivering in the snow, with their thin cobwebby garments hanging in tatters about them. Many are without shirts.... Some have their greasy coats and trousers tied around their waists with string, to prevent the piercing wind from blowing up them. A few are without shoes; and these keep one foot only to the ground."

Workhouses

From the 1830s onward, large workhouses were built to house those who could not support themselves. In many ways a workhouse resembled a Victorian prison. So that the poor would only use it as a last resort, conditions were designed to be harsher than those of the lowest-paid workers outside. Men, women, and children all lived in different wings, and the separation of families was bitterly resented.

The men broke stones, ground bones to make fertilizer, and unpicked old rope, also a punishment given to prisoners. The women cooked,

Crossing Sweepers

It was illegal to beg in Victorian Britain. To get around the law, poor boys swept the streets, asking people who crossed for money. They could be arrested for doing even this. In 1856, Jack, a fifteen-year-old London crossing sweeper told Henry Mayhew, "If there's a policeman close at hand we mustn't ask for money....We never carries no pockets, for if the policemen find us we generally pass the money to our mates, for if money's found on us we have fourteen days in prison."

Many poor children went barefoot, like two of the boys here, photographed on a London street in 1885.

cleaned, and sewed the workhouse uniforms, made of coarse linen. Charles Shaw, who as a boy in 1842 was taken to a workhouse with his family, later wrote, "We youngsters were roughly disrobed, roughly and coldly washed, and roughly attired in rough clothes, our under garments being all covered up by a rough linen pinafore. Then we parted amid bitter cries, the young ones being taken away and the parents ... taken as well to different regions."

The same system operated in the United States, where workhouses were called poorhouses. According to an 1898 newspaper article about the Boston poorhouse, in the previous year the female inmates had made 1,412 aprons, 891 dresses, 492 nightgowns, 993 petticoats, and 43 shrouds. A shroud was a plain white cotton garment worn by the dead inmates for burial.

A poor woman, dressed in rags, holding her baby.

Chapter 6: Late Victorian Fashions: 1860–1901

From the 1860s until the end of the Victorian era, women's fashions went through major changes as the crinoline fell from favor. Late-Victorian women aimed for a curving "hourglass" figure with a tiny waist and large hips and bust. This was achieved with long, shaped corsets which were tighter laced than at any time since the 1830s. The fashionable female shape also grew taller and more imposing, with high heels and hairstyles piled up on top of the head. Men's fashions, as always in the nineteenth century, saw only minor changes.

This corset shows how tightly laced women had to be to achieve an "hourglass figure."

The Bustle

In 1864 the designer Charles Frederick Worth decided that it was time to do away with the crinoline, now worn by even poor women. In its place he designed a dress which was flat at the front and sides, with a long train behind. It had a cushion padded with horsehair sewn to the back of the skirt, later called a bustle. Piled over the bustle he put a mass of cloth in folds decorated with ruffles and bows. Worth's new look made the fabric tumble behind, like a waterfall. It required far more fabric than the crinoline and it was much more impractical to wear. It was heavy, making the dress trail along the ground, and it was difficult to sit in comfortably. Worth saw the bustle and train, which was soon to be the height of fashion, as his greatest achievement. He would later boast, "I dethroned the crinoline."

Like most new women's fashions, the long, trailing dress was mocked by men. An 1867 cartoon in *Punch* shows a lady whose dress disappears behind a door. She says to a male companion, "Oh, how tiresome! Somebody must be standing on my dress! Would you just run down-stairs and see who it is Mr Brown!" In 1876 the writer John Ruskin complained, "I have lost much of the faith I once had in the common sense ... of the present race of average English women by seeing how they will allow their dresses to sweep the streets."

The bustle shrank to a small pad in the late 1870s, only to reappear in an exaggerated form in the 1880s, when it stuck out like a shelf, two feet (0.6 m) behind the wearer. This shelf was achieved with half hoops of steel bands, sewn into the lining of underskirts. Cartoons showed people resting tea trays on the shelf bustles.

These two women wear the long trailing evening dresses of the 1880s, with large padded bustles.

Relaxation for Men

While men continued to dress formally in the evening, day wear saw a shift to looser, more comfortable clothes. In 1878 *The Tailor and Cutter* trade journal complained, "We are rapidly degenerating into a slipshod state of things. After a time Frock coats and even Morning coats will be entirely a thing of the past and if things go on in this way will only be seen at museums where they will serve to amuse a wondering and awestricken group of sightseers."

Dundreary Whiskers

In the 1860s, there was a fashion for men to grow waxed moustaches with long "Dundreary" side whiskers, named after Lord Dundreary, a character played by the English actor Edward Sothern in a stage comedy, *Our American Cousin*. This was such a popular hit that it ran for almost five hundred nights in London. It was at an American performance of the play, in 1865, that President Abraham Lincoln was assassinated. Despite the assassination, Sothern continued to play the role to packed audiences until the 1880s.

Dress Reform

The late nineteenth century saw several attempts to reform the way that both men and women dressed. Some reformers claimed that Victorian clothes, especially those worn by women, were unhealthy and impractical. Others rejected them on grounds of aesthetics (concern for beauty).

Gustav Jaeger proudly models his all-woolen suit, which he promoted for health reasons.

Dr. Jaeger

Dr. Gustav Jaeger was a German zoology professor, who invented the "Sanitary Woolen System" in the 1870s. Jaeger argued that, for health reasons, all clothes should be made of wool, claiming that cotton and linen did not "breathe." He rejected trousers in favor of knee-breeches and socks, which he said were also better for the circulation. Although Jaeger's theories were scientifically incorrect, he found more followers than any other dress reformer. The most famous of them was the Irish playwright George Bernard Shaw, who wore woolen "Jaeger suits" from the 1880s until his death in 1950.

Oscar Wilde

The Irish writer Oscar Wilde was another reformer who wanted men to wear knee-breeches, though his arguments were based on aesthetics rather than health. In 1890 he wrote, "The costume of the nineteenth century is detestable. It is so sombre, so depressing." Wilde preferred the fashions of the seventeenth century, when men wore long hair and richly colored clothes with wide hats and cloaks. Describing trousers as "boring tubes," he took to wearing satin

Combinations

For underwear, Dr. Gustav Jaeger promoted knitted woolen "combinations," a body stocking which covered the body from the neck to the ankles. Jaeger claimed that the itchiness of wool against the skin stimulated blood circulation. Woolen combinations, recommended by many doctors, were widely worn from the 1880s onward. One London woman later recalled, "I still remember the childhood misery of tickly Jaeger combinations."

knee-breeches with silk stockings. Wilde was mocked in the newspapers and found few imitators. His clothes were seen as effeminate (unmanly).

Rational Dress

In 1881 two Englishwomen, Mrs. Emily King and Viscountess Harberton, formed the Rational Dress Society, dedicated to making women dress in a rational, or sensible, way. Each issue of the society's monthly gazette began with this statement: "The Rational Dress Society protests against the introduction of any fashion in dress that either deforms the figure, impedes the movements of the body, or in any way tends to injure the health. It protests against the wearing of tightly-fitting corsets; of high-heeled shoes; of heavily-weighted skirts, as rendering healthy exercise almost impossible."

The society saw dress reform as part of a wider campaign for women's right to vote, which was not won until 1920 in the United States, and 1928 in Britain. Viscountess Harberton argued that by dressing in a foolish way, women showed men that they were not sensible enough to be given the vote.

Harberton promoted the "divided skirt," a pair of baggy trousers designed to resemble a skirt. Like Amelia Bloomer before her, she was mocked for dressing in a manly way, and was once refused entrance to a hotel for wearing trousers. Only a few upper-class women were brave enough to follow her example.

An illustration from an exhibition of "rational dress" for girls and women. None of them wear tight corsets, huge bustles or trailing dresses.

New York Society

In the late nineteenth century, there were more millionaires living in New York than in any other city in the world. These were men who had grown rich by investing in new industries such as the railroads, steel, and oil. They built huge mansions along New York's Fifth Avenue, which came to be called Millionaire's Row, and their wives spent vast sums on Parisian fashions.

Easter Bonnets

From the 1870s onward, Easter Sunday was a day when the rich wore their most expensive clothes, including elaborate bonnets decorated with flowers, feathers, and ribbons, to stroll along Fifth Avenue to and from church. This grew into a tourist attraction as ordinary Americans went to Fifth Avenue to watch the rich on their "Easter Parade." In 1890 the *New York Tribune* reported, "The Easter bonnets and the Easter trousers rioted in gorgeousness.... From Madison Square to Central Park the sidewalks were rivers of beautiful raiment and happy faces." This is one Victorian custom which continues in the twenty-first century.

High Society

In Europe, the leaders of fashionable society were the royal families and nobles. The United States, however, had no royal family and no dukes or duchesses. In the late nineteenth century, upper-class Americans created their own aristocracy in which families that had been rich for generations looked down on those with "new money." Ward McAllister, who organized balls and parties, said, "With the rapid growth of riches, millionaires are too common to receive much deference.... So we have to draw social boundaries on another basis: old connections, gentle breeding."

Four Hundred

The leading figure in New York society was Mrs Caroline Astor, whose family wealth came from property development. Her ballroom was large enough to hold four

Wealthy New Yorkers spent large sums of money on French evening dresses, such as this example decorated with chrysanthemums.

Feathers

In late-Victorian New York society, it became the fashion to decorate hats with feathers from birds, including gulls, ostriches, hawks, and songbirds. Some women even wore stuffed birds on their hats. Every autumn, hundreds of thousands of wild birds were shot to adorn women's hats. Bird lovers campaigned against the fashion, which was also denounced in church by preachers. In 1898 Dr. H. M. Wharton, a Baltimore churchman, said, "It is wholesale murder.... I have commented from the pulpit frequently upon the evil of women wearing birds' wings or bodies of birds on their hats, for I have long considered it a cruel custom."

hundred guests, which was said to be the number of New Yorkers belonging to High Society. McAllister, who controlled the invitations to Astor's balls, told the press, "There are only about four hundred people in fashionable New-York society. If you go outside that number you strike people who are either not at ease in a ball-room or else make other people not at ease."

Fancy Dress

Many of the balls were costume parties, in which guests competed to wear the most inventive, luxurious, and expensive outfits. One of the most costly balls was held by Caroline Astor's great rival, Alva Vanderbilt, in March 1883. The guests included people dressed as kings, queens, famous explorers, and shepherdesses. Mrs. W. Seward Webb came as a hornet, and Alva's sister-in-law, Alice Vanderbilt, dressed as "Electric Light," the recent invention of Thomas Edison. She wore a white satin gown decorated with glistening diamonds, and a battery-operated hat with lights.

This pale, sleeveless evening gown from 1890 has a pointed waist, watered silk drapery at the back, and a sash of flowers across the bodice.

The End of the Century

In the 1890s, the clothes of both men and women grew simpler, with a greater emphasis on comfort and freedom. The impractical bustle disappeared from women's dresses. Men of all classes began to wear informal straw hats. For formal occasions, comfortable soft shirts replaced the heavily starched shirtfronts of the previous decade. In 1898 *The Tailor and Cutter* journal predicted that the starched shirtfront would be "of considerable interest to the future historian of the sartorial [clothing-related] instruments of torture of the nineteenth century."

Hats

In the 1890s, instead of wearing top hats, many men took to wearing

Cycling offered late-nineteenth-century women a new freedom, shown in the comfortable knickerbockers and relaxed poses of these Parisian ladies.

smaller hats, including straw hats, bowlers, and trilbies. The bowler was a hard, dome-shaped hat with a curled brim. It was called a derby in the United States, after the earl of Derby who made it fashionable. The trilby was a soft felt hat with a dented brim, named after a character who wore it in a popular London stage play of 1895.

In 1899 the clothing trade journal *London Tailor* complained of the decline of the top hat: "So great is the modern tendency to sacrifice appearance to comfort that before long it is feared the silk hat will only be seen in the City and Piccadilly."

Cycling

Although the Rational Dress Society's 1880s campaign to make women wear divided skirts had failed, just ten years later, women in Europe and the United States could be seen wearing knickerbockers reaching to just below the knees. The reason was the spread of a new craze for cycling. In 1896 Susan B. Anthony, an American campaigner for women's rights, said, "the bicycle has done more for the emancipation (freedom) of women than anything else in the world."

Women's bicycles were built with low crossbars, enabling them to wear skirts if they chose. Most women preferred skirts to knickerbockers, but cycling required that they were practical. Bustles and tight corsets could not be worn by cyclists. Some older people were shocked by the sight of women riding bicycles. The English novelist Eliza Lynn Linton, born in 1822, wrote, "This modern bicycling craze is not only far beyond a girl's strength but it tends to destroy the sweet simplicity of a girl's nature. Besides, how dreadful it would be if by some strange accident she were to fall off into the arms of a strange man!"

End of an Era

In 1897, as the century drew to a close, *The Tailor and Cutter* looked back at the strange fashions, such as the crinoline and the bustle, worn throughout the Victorian era. The journal predicted, "Sixty years hence we shall probably appear as ridiculous in the eyes of that generation as our ancestors appear today in ours."

The Tailor-Made

The 1890s saw the coming of the "tailor-made" for women. Modeled on the male suit, this was a close-fitting plain skirt and jacket, worn over a simple white blouse. The tailor-made was the dress of choice for the growing number of women now working in new jobs, such as secretaries, telephone operators, store assistants, and teachers. In 1898 *London Tailor* announced, "The only really new dress development which has taken place during the last half century has been the evolution of the tailor-made gown which is doubtless due to the active life now led by women of every class."

Timeline

1829 Sir Robert Peel founds the first professional police force, whose officers wear uniforms modeled on those of servants.

1830 Joseph Palmer shocks the town of Fitchburg, Connecticut, by growing a beard.

1833 Walter Hunt invents the first practical sewing machine.

1837 Queen Victoria comes to the throne.

1840 Wearing a white dress, Queen Victoria marries Prince Albert.

1846 Elias Howe patents his sewing machine.

1846–52 The first department stores open in Paris, New York, and Newcastle.

1849 Walter Hunt invents the safety pin.

1851 The Great Exhibition in Britain includes displays of fashion and textiles.
Amelia Bloomer promotes a trouser costume for women.
Isaac Merritt Singer produces an improved sewing machine.

1854–6 The Crimean War, in which Britain, France, and Turkey fight Russia, leads to the introduction of looser tunics for the military.

1856 The steel-hooped crinoline is invented.
William Perkin makes the first artificial dye, from coal tar.

1857 Charles Frederick Worth opens the first haute couture business, in Paris.

1860 John Barron uses the band knife to cut several layers of cloth at once.

1861 The death of Prince Albert. Queen Victoria goes into mourning dress. Knee breeches are now worn by men for walking in the country.

1861–5 The American Civil War, fought by the North in dark blue and the South in gray uniforms.

1864 The first dresses with bustles are made.

1870s Crinoline makers go out of business.

1881 The first war between Britain and the Boers, in which British soldiers fight in scarlet jackets.
The Rational Dress Society is founded, to reform women's clothing.

1883 The wide "shelf bustle" becomes fashionable.

1885 The publication of *Little Lord Fauntleroy* leads to a fashion for boys' velvet knee-breeches.

1888 John Dunlop invents inflatable bicycle tires. The resulting cycling craze makes it acceptable for women to wear knee-breeches.
The first Sears Roebuck mail-order catalog is produced.

1892 The zip fastener is invented by Whitcomb Judson.

1899 – 1900 The Second Boer War, with British soldiers now fighting in khaki uniforms.

1901 The death of Queen Victoria.

Glossary

boater A round straw hat with a flat brim and narrow flat crown, originally based on those worn by sailors.

bowler A hard felt hat with a narrow brim and a round crown.

bustle A pad or frame worn at the back of a dress, to make the rear stick out.

calico Coarse light cotton, used for underwear and shirts, named after Calcutta, India, its place of origin.

combinations Body-stocking underwear, so called because it combined vest and leggings.

corduroy A hard-wearing, ridged cotton fabric worn by laborers. Its name derives from the French *corde du roy* (king's cord).

cravat Elaborate neckwear worn by men in the early 1800s. A long band of folded muslin was wrapped around the neck and tied in a knot or bow.

crepe A dull, crinkled black silk fabric, worn for mourning. Also spelled *crape*.

crinoline Originally a petticoat stiffened with horsehair (*crin* in French). From 1856 onward, the word was applied to the cage crinoline, made of steel hoops.

denim A tough cotton fabric, woven from two different-colored threads, with a twill, or diagonal, weave. The name comes from *Serge de Nimes* (Nimes Serge).

evening dress Formal dress worn for social occasions, such as dinners and balls, in the evenings. Men wore white shirts and ties with black tailcoats and trousers, while women wore low-cut dresses with jewelry.

felt A fabric with matted fibers, usually animal hairs.

frock coat A long men's jacket with a square front.

jean A tough twilled material made from wool and cotton, used for work wear, and named after Genoa, Italy.

knickerbockers Loose-fitting knee-breeches, named after Washington Irving's 1809 book, *Knickerbocker's History of New York*, which has illustrations of such clothes worn by seventeenth-century Dutch settlers.

linen A fabric made from the fibers of the flax plant.

morning coat A men's coat with tails, worn in the daytime. Unlike a black evening coat, which had a cutaway square front, a morning coat had a curved front and came in various colors.

morning dress Formal daywear worn by men and women.

mourning The period following the death of a loved one, when special dark clothes were worn to show sorrow.

muslin A fine, delicately woven cotton fabric.

navvy A laborer building railroads and canals. The name is short for *navigator*.

satin A glossy fabric made from silk.

shoddy A cheap fabric made by tearing up old cloth and mixing it with new fibers.

silk A fine, strong, soft fabric made from the cocoons spun by silkworms.

smock A long, loose, thick shirt, usually cotton, worn by farm laborers and other manual workers.

spin Draw out and twist fibers, such as wool or cotton, to make thread.

starch Vegetable extracts used to stiffen material, such as shirtfronts and collars.

stays Another name for corsets.

tailor-made A woman's suit, with simple jacket and skirt, worn in the late nineteenth century.

top hat A formal black hat, made from felt or silk, with a high crown.

trilby A soft felt hat with a brim and a dent in the top, named after a character in an 1895 stage play by George du Maurier.

tweed A tough, thick woolen cloth with a diagonal weave, originally from Scotland. Its name comes from a misreading of the word *twill*, spelt *tweel* on a bill.

twill A diagonal weave, which gives fabrics extra strength.

weave To form cloth by interlacing threads from two different directions. Lengthwise, or warp, threads are stretched on a frame called a loom. A second thread, the weft, is then passed from side to side.

whipcord A tough wool fabric with raised ridges.

Further Information

Adult Reference Sources

Bradfield, Nancy, *Costume in Detail: Women's Dress, 1730-1930* (Eric Dobby Publishing, 1998)

Cosgrave, Bronwyn, *Costume and Fashion: A Complete History* (Hamlyn, 2003)

Gernsheim, Alison, *Victorian and Edwardian Fashion: A Photographic Survey* (Dover Publications, 1982)

Grafton, Carol, *Victorian Fashions: A Pictorial Archive* (Dover Publications, 1999)

Young Adult Reference Sources

Nunn, Joan, *Fashion in Costume 1200-2000* (A & C Black, 2000)

Goodwin, Jane, *All about the Victorians* (Hodder Wayland, 2001)

Kramer, Anne, *Eyewitness Guide: The Victorians* (Dorling Kindersley, 2003)

Langley, Andrew, *Victorian Britain* (Heinemann Library, 1994)

Internet Resources

http://www.fashion-era.com/victorians.htm
All about Victorian society, with numerous sections on fashion and costume.

http://www.lahacal.org/gentleman/behavior.html
The Gentleman's Page: A Practical Guide for the Nineteenth-Century American Man.

http://www.speel.demon.co.uk/other/grtexhib.htm
The Great Exhibition of 1851.

http://www.charlesfrederickworth.org
Charles Frederick Worth.

http://www.hairarchives.com/private/victorian 1new.htm
Women's hair in Victorian times. Includes archive photographs.

http://www.pemberley.com/janeinfo/victcfsh.html
Slightly silly Victorian fashions.

http://www.fathom.com/course/21701726/session1.html
The Secret History of the Corset and Crinoline.

http://www.rogerco.freeserve.co.uk/
Victorian and Edwardian photographs.

http://www.costumes.org/history/100pages/victlinks.htm
Victorian fashion links.

http://www.fashion-era.com/the_victorian_era.htm
Fashion Era: The Victorian Era.

http://www.fashionera.com/the_victorian_era.htm
Eras of Elegance: Victorian.

http://histclo.hispeed.com/
Historical boys clothing.

http://www.fabrics.net/joan800.asp
Vintage Fabric: A History of Sweatshops.

http://www.geocities.com/victorianlace11/mourning.html
"The Mourning After:" Victorian Mourning Customs.

http://www.costumes.org/classes/fashiondress/dress_reformblip.htm
Victorian dress reform links.

Index